The Dramatic Silences of His Last Week

The Dramatic Silences of His Last Week

WHEATON PHILLIPS WEBB

Abingdon Press
Nashville   New York

THE DRAMATIC SILENCES OF HIS LAST WEEK

ISBN 0-687-11231-1

Library of Congress Catalog Card Number: 74-173949

MANUFACTURED BY THE PARTHENON PRESS AT
NASHVILLE, TENNESSEE, UNITED STATES OF AMERICA

for Alice

The Caterpillar and Alice looked
at each other for some time in silence.
Lewis Carroll, "Alice's Adventures in Wonderland"

Sometimes, in dark caves, men have gone
to the edge of unspeaking precipices,
and, wondering what was the depth,
have cast down fragments of rock,
and listened for the report of their fall,
that they might judge how deep that blackness was;
and listening—still listening—
no sound returns; no sullen plash, no clinking
stroke as of rock against rock—nothing but silence,
utter silence! And so I stand upon
the precipice of life. I sound the depths of the
other world with curious inquiries.
But from it comes no echo and no answer
to my questions. No analogies can grapple and
bring up from the depths of the darkness of
the lost world the probable truths.
No philosophy has line and plummet long enough
to sound the depths. There remains for
us only the few authoritative and solemn words of God.
                                Henry Ward Beecher

Contents

Preface

**How calm a moment may precede
One that shall thrill the world for ever!**
Alfred Domett

Repeatedly during the final week of our Lord's ministry an abrupt silence falls, arresting a mounting crisis as if eternity were momentarily frozen in time.

You enter an upper room where bread and wine have become sacrament. It is like the thrust of a sword as Jesus announces that the hand of a betrayer rests on the table beside his own. You catch your breath at the silence that closes around the Twelve as in sorrow they search the face of their Lord, aware that the secrets of their hearts are no longer private.

Underneath the olive trees of a garden soldiers appear out of the darkness, their lanterns and torches eerie in this place of shadows. Suddenly Jesus stands revealed before them, armed with innocence. Awed by his presence, the soldiers crouch back, aghast and mute, their faces hidden underneath the trees.

In the bleak stillness of dawn a cock crows twice. But it is not a signal for heroic action. Instead, a hushed sobbing as a man disappears down the gray road.

You enter a palace where Jesus stands indicted and wait to hear his eloquent defense. The words remain unspoken.

You stand before a cross praying that as once before the heavens will be vocal with the vindication: *This is my beloved Son.* Instead, silence and darkness until the ninth hour, and you wait for three days in silent grief with those who had trusted that he would redeem Israel.

You see a man give himself away by the manner in which he takes a loaf of bread in his hands and breaks it; but at that moment. . . .

Are the silences that punctuate the crises of these hours preserved for us by the wisdom of God so that we may be still and observe the profiles of men suddenly mute, and so understand and believe?

If we permit these incidents to become a prompter's script for our own self-examination before Christ, is it possible that they will prepare us to look lovingly upon our Lord, that we may enter into communion with his spirit, and so learn anew to live?

The Silence in the City

And those who went before and those
who followed cried out, "Hosanna! . . .
Hosanna in the highest!"
And he entered Jerusalem, and went into the
temple; and when he had looked round
at everything, as it was already late, he went
out to Bethany with the twelve.
Mark 11:9-11

A deep silence also, and a kind of deadly
night, had seized upon the city.
Josephus, "Wars of the Jews."

Do you sense the abrupt change in the sky as the long
shadows of late afternoon begin to wrap as in a mantle the
scenes of the Triumphal Entry? The day had begun with
eager disciples and throngs of pilgrims following Jesus
along the white road that winds from Bethany over the
Mount of Olives. Hearts are exultant for it is the time of
the promise.

A bend in the road, and the tawny walls of Jerusalem
rise on their vision just beyond the brook Kidron, this
Jerusalem that is more than a city set on a hill. It is the
sacred community of their highest expectations. Yet, if

you look again, it is not so much spread before them as above them, situated just beyond that white cloud stealing across the sky, a city coming down from God out of heaven. It is so these patriots see their nation's capital and body forth their covenant with God.

Now the golden dome of the temple flashes in the sun, the smoke from the altar a white plume against the dazzling blue of the sky. Suddenly the pilgrims break into a great shout which goes flailing up against the hills:

"Hosanna!
Blessed be he who comes in the name of the Lord!—
Blessed be the kingdom of our father David
that is coming!"

We are likely to picture the Triumphal Entry as a victorious climax in the life of our Lord, a reprieve before the final desolation of the cross. Actually, for him it was a day of sorrow, and we never begin to penetrate his heart until we see through his eyes that ancient city where it lay "like a face seamed with old suffering," and again in its day of visitation before another generation has passed, with its broken walls, its temple in ruins, and its little children starved to death.

One moment you hear the glad shouts of the Galileans, their hearts pounding with messianic hopes—the next, silence and a vanished glory. He has entered the temple, has passed into an inner court. The shouts of the Galileans have become a murmur of distant seas, at last have ceased.

In that silence he "looked round at everything"—at the mysterious curtain that shrouded the Holy of Holies, at the solid-seeming pillars, at the smoking altar. He looked down the unrepenting years and unashamedly wept over the city.

The palms wither on the road. The little beast on which he had ridden into the city, dramatizing a prophet's vision, has been led away. This day, which promised to be one of the signal days of history when the disciples stood on the threshold of a kingdom, ends with a man walking through the dusk of the temple, solitary and alone. It is one of the surprising silences of his last week.

This stillness that enfolds our Lord after the clamor of a turbulent day shatters our own complacency. For you never quite disabuse your mind of the suspicion that it is here in the silence that God has something to say to us we failed to hear amid the hosannas.

Let the shouting and the tumult die, let approval be withdrawn and our first successes suffer reversal, let enthusiasm cool when risk is demanded of it—and the Triumphal Entry becomes the prelude to a tragic exit. It is at such an hour when failure threatens that for the first time many a man has had the courage to look clairvoyantly into the mystery of his own destiny and to realize how cheap are many of the vaulting ambitions that commandeer his soul.

It is here that temptation insinuates itself, yet without betraying its hand. Turn these stones into bread, and multitudes will take up arms for you. Throw yourself down from the pinnacle of the temple, and the astounded populace will recognize you as their king. Behold the kingdoms of the world—they are yours if you will fall down and worship the lord of these kingdoms. A procession that does not stop at the temple but marches on proclaiming nationalism its god—salute this, and there will be no end to the adulation. The souls you cry out to save, the land you would deliver from the iron hand of Rome—do you not see that they are ready to rise at your command and free the city of your fathers?

But he would not. Men were to be his companions "out of love and devotion or not at all." It is when we see this lonely Christ moving through his Father's house in a mantle of stillness and brooding on the dooms men will bring upon themselves and on their children that we begin to feel a hollowness in our own being that cries out, "What one thing must I do to be saved?"

The omens which the poet Heine detected blowing in the wind in 1834 and which he offered as "consolation to his disappointed revolutionary friends" reappear but slightly altered today:

The revolution will come, and it will be no milk and water affair. . . . The followers of Kant with their lack of reverence for everything, the followers of Fichte with their fanaticism of the will are bound to make a thorough job of it. . . .

Christianity—and this is its fairest merit—subdued to a certain extent the brutal warrior ardor of the Germans, but it could not entirely quench it; and when the Cross, that restraining talisman, falls to pieces, there will break forth again the ferocity of the old combatants, the frantic Berserker rage of which northern poets have said and sung. The talisman has become rotten, and the day will come when it will pitifully crumble to dust. The old stone gods will then arise from the forgotten ruins and wipe from their eyes the dust of centuries, and Thor with his giant hammer will arise again, and he will crush the Gothic cathedrals. . . . Smile not at the fantasy of one who foresees in the region of reality the same outburst of revolution that has taken place in the region of the intellect.

The thought precedes the deed as lightning with thunder. . . .
And *the hour will come.*[1]

It is as if our Lord were riding again into our midst and saying to us, "If you had only known, on this great day, the way that leads to peace! But no; it is hidden from your sight."

We set great store by summit conferences. But there is one summit to which we are reluctant to turn. We see the whole earth threatened and seek one landmark that will tower above the wrecks of time. All that remains at the summit is his Cross—the broken and the contrite heart.

It is curious how the Cross continues to haunt us with the recollection of what our deepest intuitions instruct us we were meant to be.

Above the high altar of the Benedictine Abbey of Ampleforth, in Yorkshire, hung a man. He was holding on precariously to the foot of the crucifix, while a voice said: "*Amplexus expecta* (Cling and wait)!"

Thus Professor Arnold Toynbee once saw himself in a dream. The eminent British historian (who dreams as fluently in Latin as he writes in Greek) tells this nighttime vision in the concluding volumes of his monumental *Study of History.* While to twentieth century psychoanalysts the dream may be a commonplace of troubled souls, it nevertheless sums up Historian Toynbee's message to Western civilization. The message is: hang on, wait and pray . . . the mind that formed (the words), the context in which they are set down and the view of man that lies behind them, all compel utmost attention from Americans, who themselves are now haunted by the feeling that they are precariously hanging on above a menacing chasm of history.[2]

Christ had the courage to fail. He failed to become the embodiment of the national hopes—the Zealots with their passion for violence could do that. He failed to withdraw from the society of the sinful and the broken—the Essenes could do that. He failed to be identified with the juiceless and joyless authority of the establishment—the Pharisees could do that.

For him it was a lonelier road, a stripping away at last of even his seamless robe, but to the last a fierce and unyielding faith in the magnificent failure of his solitary purpose.

You see him in the shadowy inner court of the temple as he realizes that for the last time he is "looking round at everything"—his Father's house, the ancient city, the faces of many he had loved and by his love had healed. And as it was already late, he went out to Bethany with the Twelve.

> The window-sills are empty; no crowds wait;
> Here at the pavement's edge I watch alone.
> Master, like sunlight strike my slaty heart
> And ask not acclamations from the stone.[3]

The Silence at the Table

When it was evening,
he sat at table with the twelve disciples;
and as they were eating, he said,
"Truly, I say to you,
one of you will betray me."
And they were very sorrowful,
and began to say to him, one after another,
"Is it I, Lord?"
Matthew 26:20-22

Where silence is, man is
observed by silence. Silence looks at
man more than man looks at silence.
Man does not put silence to the test!
Silence puts man to the test.
Max Picard, "The World of Silence."

If you had ever seen the face of Jesus through the steam of Martha's kitchen, or mirrored in the blue of Galilee, or framed in the doorway of the house of the widow of Nain, you would have fallen into the habit of looking for him, and would gladly have stood at the side of the goodman of the house as he watched Jesus and the Twelve approach his door. This goodman lives in our memory because he threw open a door for Christ. With his own hands, I like to think, he had trimmed the lamp which would light the table where our Lord will gather with his own.

Ever since the goodman of the house laid white linen for the coming of Jesus and the disciples to the Upper Room, the Lord's Table has provided a place where those who seek the fellowship of the mystery might be at one with Christ.

A table where a family gathers in weariness, or in hope, or in loving communion is not too humble a place for Christ to be present. He comes to us, the doors being shut. He is known to us in the breaking of bread. When he feeds the multitudes, are not we of the company?

Dusk descends as the disciples and their Lord gather about the table. What cups did each remember as the Passover moon slid above the casement of a window in the Upper Room? Did Judas remember a cup that had gone the rounds where traitors conspired the death of beauty for thirty pieces of silver? Did the Beloved Disciple recall the wind's song on a country road, and a cup of cold water given to a man athirst? Did Jesus remember the stillness of a house at Nazareth in the silence of the sleeptime and Mary bringing a cup all brimming with her love to a feverish child at midnight?

In his alienation one man rejects the cup life offers him; another dashes his cup to the floor in anger; yet another fills his cup with a drug and suspends memory. Jesus took the cup and gave thanks. It was his own life trembling there in his hand. In despair, he might have "let this cup pass" and renounced this desolate course which could only lead to the green hill far away. Instead, he passed his cup down the table: *"This is my blood of the covenant, which is poured out for many."*

Like the one who had sung the Song of the Cup long before, we find that our own cups are running over and spill red down the cloth. God's love pulses through the heart of a man, brims over, flows red from his side, down, down, until it dyes the cross with crimson. Beyond this tree of the knowledge of good and evil the roads are not open unless he opens them.

Darkness falls over the Upper Room. Darkness falls upon our world. But that strange Man with the cup in his hands holds the secrets of the broken hearts of all the generations locked in his own. No man need thrust a spear into his side to prove that the love of God is there.

While they were eating, Jesus said, "Truly I say to you, one of you will betray me." As the scene rises on your mind, you become aware that every motion in the room has abruptly ceased. The tension at the table is at the breaking point. The unnatural calm, the "aghast silence" that falls upon the fellowship is the measure of each man's uncompromising knowledge of himself.

"And they were very sorrowful, and began to say to him, one after another, 'Is it I, Lord?' " (Matt. 26:22). The hand of the betrayer is among the hands that rest on the cloth near the hand of Jesus, but our Lord gives to each disciple the cup and breaks for each the sacramental loaf. Yet in that momentary silence when time is suspended, each man's eyes are on the face of Christ, each looks into himself and trembles at the heart's capacity for betrayal of the highest.

Strange, that in exalted moments when vision has been

purified, the will made strong, or a great troth plighted, a shadow falls, and the heart becomes an abyss we cannot plumb. "For from within, out of the heart of man, come evil thoughts, fornication, theft, murder, adultery, coveting, wickedness, deceit, licentiousness, envy, slander, pride, foolishness. All these evil things come from within, and they defile a man" (Mark 7:21-22).

To know this is the beginning of the true Lent of the spirit. To know it is to disavow an easy optimism, and to be thrown back in penitence on the mercy of God. Each time that we bow at his Table we acknowledge that God is doing something for us and in us that we cannot do for ourselves: he is bringing us face to face with a Redeemer, whose presence we find in comradeships of the forgiving and the forgiven. Nothing can annul the rancor, the pride, the prejudices that explode in war except there be such a fellowship of the mystery.

Above the altar of the John Hus Presbyterian Church in Binghamton, New York, there is a window in which the chalice of the Last Supper rests upon a Bible. As I slowly walked down the aisle toward the altar, the chalice appeared to be filling with wine. At last, a little startled by this mystery, when I knelt, I saw that the chalice was full to the brim.

The pastor of the church had designed the window himself, and was, of all his congregation, the most surprised when a boy one day pointed out to him the strange way in which the chalice filled as one approached it.

"I am not sure of the reason," he told me, "but I think that from the light refracted from the purple cover of the Bible on which the cup rests, and because of the angle at which you see it when you are on your knees, the cup is full—and about to run over like that other cup in the Twenty-third Psalm."

There are wisdoms that are ours only when we are on our knees, and one of these William Blake has noted:

> And throughout all Eternity
> I forgive you, you forgive me.
> As our dear Redeemer said:
> "This is the Wine, and this the Bread." [1]

Afterward, the goodman of the house would surely remember the hands he had seen upon his table: the calloused hands of the fishermen; the twitch of Iscariot's fingers as one piece of silver clinks against another in his pocket; the hands of Jesus, strong as a carpenter's, sure as a physician's—hands across a table to make or mar the world.

My dear friend, the Rev. Charles Gilbert, once related his memories of treasured moments as he administered the Sacrament in our village church:

"I am thinking of the hands on the chancel railing. Another group of communicants kneels, and I give to each the bread and wine. It is the end of summer. Here is one of our staunch farm women. I know how her hands became stained. She was pulling weeds from her kitchen garden yesterday. Those stains do not come off overnight. She takes the bread.

"The hands of the man kneeling next to her are thick and stubby, grimy with ground-in grease. He is a blacksmith. His hands are always like this when I give him the cup of the New Covenant. But there was a time when his hands were pale. He had been ill for two months. Those are hard days for the family of a blacksmith when he is shut in the house and wishes he could go back to work. I would rather see the healthy grime of toil than the strange whiteness of the hands of those who have long been ill.

"Here is a man, bent and white-haired. I hold the cup to him. His hands tremble. He is visiting his children today and worshiping in the church of his youth. His children now are grown. Many of them have families of their own who are numbered with our most loyal families. I honor this trembling father: *This is my body which is broken for you.*

"Now I bend down to give the cup to tiny hands that reach up—*Suffer the little chlidren to come unto me*—little hands of children that can squeeze the world so hard."

If this revealing love which the Christ of God has shed abroad in our hearts should be ignored, and a generation should rise indifferent to his ethical demands, a silence of a different order would fall upon our world. "There is a silence that is not 'golden': the silence of unbelief, indifferent and sullen; the silence of diffidence, timorous and hesitating." [2]

I sometimes think that the loneliest question in all literature was Jesus' question: *Will you also go away?* Did you ever ponder his gracious words of the resurrection and the life, and of the vine and the branches, or listen to our Lord's prayer of intercession, and mark that Judas had not stayed to hear him speak of these high matters? Jesus and the Eleven sang a hallel, a psalm of praise to God, but Judas was not there to join in it. Holy Communion there had been, but at the last one was absent.

One Maundy Thursday night when a storm was sweeping down out of the north country, I administered the

Lord's Supper in the candlelight of a village church. Only twelve had braved the great drifts of snow to be present. When they had gone and silence settled upon the church, I observed the fragments of sacramental bread that remained on the altar and the sacramental wine prepared for others who had not come.

Perhaps it was a recollection of St. Francis who loved life on the wing that prompted me to lay the broken fragments of the bread on the branches of a spruce outside my study window and to pour the wine beside it.

On the dawn of Good Friday the sun rose in blinding beauty upon the snowy earth, and I saw much miracle as men have seldom dreamed since the Middle Ages: my tree, one symphony of singing birds, had turned Christ's body into song. And where I poured the rich libation sprang in the heat of a summer yet to come the poppy's scarlet cup.

If all earth's children were to deny their Lord, the stones would cry out of the wall, the birds of the air lift their voices, and the flowers of the field proclaim him King of kings and Lord of lords.

The Silence at the Oil Press

When he said to them,
"I am he," they drew back and
fell to the ground.
John 18:6

"Does a man dare speak here?"
"If you can improve the silence."
From a Quaker meeting

Often in imagination we have followed our Lord and his disciples from the Upper Room, leaving the goodman of the house to close the door. Like the young man dressed in white linen who secretly followed Jesus into the Garden of Gethsemane, we too will keep a reverent distance as we slip after the disciples through the hushed streets of Jerusalem.

Under the full Passover moon the old city casts the long shadow of its eastern wall into the gaunt ravine where the brook Kidron, a winter torrent, is sometimes still swollen with a freshet at this season. Jesus and the Eleven take the stony road that plunges down steeply into the gorge through the walled orchards and gardens and crosses the Kidron on the great viaduct whose double arches were talisman against defilement from the dead who slept below.

If they talked at all, was it in whispered apprehension that events were pushing rapidly toward a climax? What memories stirred in the mind of Jesus as he approached the bridge? Was it here that he may have spoken the words attributed to him in a curious inscription on the gate of a mosque in India? "The world is only a bridge. You may pass over it, but do not build your dwellings upon it." [1]

A strange little bridge, this, for "it was over this viaduct that the 'red heifer,' the sin-offering of the nation, was led to death, and it was also this way that the scapegoat— surely the most pitiful symbol of a nation's transgressions —was taken on the Day of Atonement and sent by relays of men into the wilderness, where he was cast from a rock." [2]

The black Kidron "was no pleasant stream. The sacrificial blood wherewith the Temple's altars were sprinkled, drained into it, and it was running red with the blood of paschal lambs as the lamb of God passed over it." [3]

As we follow our Lord and his disciples, we climb in the shivering darkness the lower slopes of the Mount of Olives beyond the Kidron. Looking down from the heights of Olivet on Jerusalem and the white marble of the temple, pale in the moon's dim light, Jesus had once spoken to Peter and Andrew, James and John of the end of the age and of the destruction of the city. Here they had watched the stars write their inscrutable mysteries in the sky and had asked him the questions that cut deep into destiny. Here too he had spoken to them of a kingdom not made with hands which was already in their midst and which would yet come with power.

Here, we may presume, the man with the pitcher of water who had guided the disciples by a secret way to the Upper Room, and Joseph of Arimathea, as yet the undeclared, and Nicodemus, confirmed in old habit; here the other Mary and the humble of heart who had seen in Jesus the hope of a better age had met sometimes. Judas who betrayed him knew the place, for Jesus had often held tryst with his disciples there. So they came to Gethsemane.

Each one who walks this road in imagination will know in his own heart how far he may trespass upon this garden. Some of us will be reluctant to go beyond the gate, and for the majority of the disciples on that fateful night this was true. A smaller number may join the three who were bidden to proceed a short way along the path. But there is One here who must go to the heart of the garden, whither no man may follow.

In this garden there was an oil press of roughhewn stone for crushing olives. It was from the oil press that the garden received its name—Gethsemane. It must have been near this stone trough that Jesus knelt to pray, *"Father, if it be thy will, take this cup from me"*—his face wet with sweat that betrayed the agony of his great decision.

As he prayed, with his hand perhaps resting on the cold stone trough of the oil press, it must have been clear to him that for a dedicated life, as for the ripe fruit of the olive, its virtue issues only in its refusal to save itself. When you see Christ facing the cross beside that oil press, you come very close to touching the hem of the vesture of God.

A sudden clamor of voices, and you hear the tramp of heavy boots crossing the Kidron. Through the trees the flaming torches in the hands of soldiers light the faces of a small company led by Judas.

Our Lord is erect now, standing by the oil press, visible in his seamless robe beneath a gnarled olive tree, a tall figure, regal.

"Whom do you seek?"

"We seek Jesus of Nazareth."

"I am he."

You feel that it would have been appropriate if something full of beauty and terror here had lighted up the night. Instead, a silence, ominous and breathless, freezes the hearts of the soldiers as they draw away from him and fall to the ground, cowering into the shadows, overawed by the presence of Jesus as he stands, like a visitor from other worlds, in the solitary purity of his commanding purpose.

What shall we say of a moment like this? For this is a silence that belongs to something larger than worlds of space and time. What is here portrayed is revealingly and everlastingly true: Through the gospel we are permitted to see our Lord in that more-than-human stature in which the apostles were the first to proclaim him and in which our own faith is bound to confess him.

In Christ we see one whose purity soars above us like a white flame. He is one of us—and yet remote. "No man ever spoke like this man!" So, on an earlier occasion, the officers who had been dispatched to seize Jesus had offered their alibi for not laying hand on him. "Truly this man was a son of God!" So, one of his crucifiers was to confess in awe, an admission into which we read our own larger faith as we see the Christ stand.

Others there have been whose fearlessness in Christ silenced their enemies, who like the soldiers in the Garden of the Oil Press fell back before the astonishing presence of Christ.

It is told of Bunyan that once, when a body of constables entered the house where he was preaching and one of them was ordered to arrest him, he fixed his eyes steadfastly on the man, holding the while an open Bible in his hand. The constable turned pale and fell back. "See," cried Bunyan, looking round upon the company, "how this man trembleth at the Word of God!" And it is told of John Wesley that once, in the days of his persecution, he was beset on the street by a gang of ruffians. "Which is he? which is he?" they cried, uncertain of their victim amid the throng. "I am he," said the man of God, stepping forward and facing them undaunted; and they retreated in amazement. And what marvel is it that His assailants bowed before the majesty of the Son of Man? It had overawed the lawless Nazarenes, and stayed their wild hands when they would have hurled Him over the precipice; and what marvel is it that now in Gethsemane, amid the weird shadows of the night, this band should quail in His presence?" [4]

Again Jesus asked them, *"Whom do you seek?"*
And they said, "Jesus of Nazareth."
"I told you that I am he; so, if you seek me, let these men go," with a gesture toward the trapped disciples.

There is the sudden glint of reflected torches on the steel of Peter's sword. The silence snaps in a moment. Yet that silence speaks more surely than any clamorous tongue that profaned Gethsemane that "the dethroned powers that rule," though they have their hour and the power of darkness, do not have the Day.

The soldiers remember their old duties, recover from their astonishment, and seize Christ. But that moment when they cowered back and fell to the ground in silence before him is prophetic of a day when before him every knee shall bow and every tongue confess that he is not only Lord of the Garden of the Oil Press but of the confessing hearts of men in all the earth.

The Silence by the Fire

At that moment, while he was
still speaking, a cock crew; and
the Lord turned and looked at Peter.
And Peter remembered . . .
Luke 22:60-61 NEB

Jesus himself spoke in short aphorisms
and oracles and tightly knit parables,
but also, we may say, in silences.
Amos N. Wilder, "The Language of the Gospel."

Niels Bohr, one of the elite group of atomic scientists whose calculations produced the bomb, once visited Kronberg castle, connected with the Hamlet legend. As he pondered the gloomy pile where Shakespeare had set his tragedy, Bohr said:

Isn't it strange how this castle changes as soon as one imagines that Hamlet lived here? . . . The stones, the wood carvings in the church, constitute the whole castle. None of this should be changed by the fact that Hamlet lived here, and yet. . . . Suddenly the walls and ramparts speak quite a different language. The courtyard becomes an entire world, a dark corner reminds us of a dark corner in the human soul . . . Kronberg becomes quite a different castle for us.[1]

So another courtyard, that of Caiaphas the high priest, becomes "quite a different courtyard for us" because our Lord once looked down upon it from the portico where he was held prisoner.

A moth irresistibly attracted to a flame that will singe it —this is Peter warming his hands as he sits in the circle huddled around the charcoal fire in the courtyard. Whatever the conflict in his soul—perhaps between a hesitant loyalty and hope of a rescue—here are materials for drama of a different order.

Let the picture rise on your imagination: the sentries pacing the portico above, the shivering servants warming their numbed fingers below in the dull glow of the coals, a serving-maid flitting past. The fire blazes up for an instant, and her sharp eyes catch a glimpse of the stranger.

"You were there too, with this man from Nazareth, this Jesus!"

"I know nothing! I don't know what you mean!"

The sky is imperceptibly changing to a dove's wing in the east. Peter shrinks into the darkness and slips out into the forecourt. But here the serving-maid spies him again. Somewhere a cock is crowing, bidding the sun rise over Jordan.

"Oh, he's one of them!" the maid insists again to the by-standers.

"No, I'm not."

But they detect the guttural of his Galilean accent.

"Surely you're one of them. You must be! You're a Galilean!"

And now his heart is pounding. He breaks out in the

curses that betray the face of his fear: "I don't know this man you speak of!"

But the words have scarcely died on his lips when the sound of a cock crowing falls a second time on his ears. Through a door opening on the portico above a lamp illuminates the figure of Jesus dressed in the festal garments of the Last Supper, his wrists bound. Jesus turns and looks straight at him. And Peter remembered . . .

The sudden silence that falls over the courtyard and over the shuddering apostle goes like a knife through the heart. That silence and that mute, searching look in the eyes of Jesus constitute one of the great emotional crises in the Gospels.

Someone has suggested that Jesus was looking at Peter "as he had looked at him on that never-forgotten day when they first met. In those two looks of Jesus is written the history of Peter's soul." [2] He had come many leagues since Andrew his brother had introduced him to Jesus. Jesus had looked him in the eyes then and had said, *So you are Simon the son of John? You shall be called the Rock."* (See John 1:42, *n.*)

There would be a time when the shadow of Peter passing by would carry healing, but that was after— Now Peter is immersed in the shadow of himself in the solitude of his failure and the total collapse of his courage. You look at him and it suddenly strikes you: I could have done that!

But it belongs to the glory of the Gospel that the Christ who gave himself for us keeps looking straight at us, undiscouraged, and with a look that sees into the heart, but sees more—sees possibilities of which the heart is not yet capable, but which it may yet achieve.

It is something that Peter, the man of the sea, should have felt on that night in the courtyard that the fate of Christ was in his hands. It is something that, having failed in the final troth, he went out and wept bitterly. Cockcrow —and silence. Yet so long as the soul remains capable of understanding such a silence as this, the future of a man is not without hope.

For there are silences in which the soul discovers itself— discovers that it is impossible to betray another without betraying itself. All through the years these silences will fall unexpectedly upon us like a gentle hand laid upon our shoulder, suddenly arresting us and awakening memory.

> There is the silence of a great hatred,
> And the silence of a great love,
> And the silence of a deep peace of mind,
> And the silence of an embittered friendship,
> There is the silence of a spiritual crisis,
> Through which your soul, exquisitely tortured,
> Comes with visions not to be uttered
> Into a realm of higher life. . . .
>
> There is the silence of defeat.
> There is the silence of those unjustly punished;
> And the silence of the dying whose hand
> Suddenly grips yours.
> There is the silence between father and son,
> When the father cannot explain his life,
> Even though he be misunderstood for it. . . .
>
> And there is the silence of age,
> Too full of wisdom for the tongue to utter it
> In words intelligible to those who have not lived
> The great range of life.
>
> Edgar Lee Masters, "Silence"

Peter fled from the fire and from the unbearable silence after cockcrow, overwhelmed with failure. But it is scarcely failure when out of profound introspection a man enlists anew and holds steadily to his purpose, at last to offer his life for the Christ who has claimed him. For there was yet a third time when Jesus was to look at Peter, that moment when the risen Master appeared to him and so confirmed that a man can rise out of his missed chances and his spoiled yesterdays, and in truth be the Rock.

Those who abide in Christ are being changed day by day. They put behind them the things that are past. They press on for the prize of the high calling. They enter into newness of life. They inherit a kingdom not made with hands. They have heard the cock crow twice—but they have also seen his crucifixion. We too have seen his crucifixion, and have become men of hope.

It is now many years since I saw Frederick Wight's painting, "The Modern Crucifixion" one summer day in a little white church at Chatham on Cape Cod. The painting depicts the Crucifixion in contemporary American dress against a background of New England cliff and sea. The figures in the picture were posed by residents of Chatham —fisherfolk, and their wives and children.

The moment pictured is when Christ, with head erect, and without a sign of physical or mental anguish, turns to the repentant thief with the triumphant words, *"Today thou shalt be with me in paradise."* The figure of a young girl in blue stands at the left of Christ, looking earnestly at him. On the opposite side his mother sits at the foot of the cross.

In the background a soldier in khaki uniform prevents a

group of disciples from completing their ascent to the top of the cliff.

The cross of the repentant thief leans symbolically toward the Master's cross. The unrepentant thief who challenged Christ is here portrayed not as a hardened criminal, rather as one of a thousand disinterested people who heed only the phenomenal or fanatical leadership. So, in a side drama, this indifferent man is grouped with his family. His wife holds up her baby in desperate hope that some miracle may save the crucified, yet resigns herself to face the adjustments of a broken home. In back of them by the sea one catches a glimpse of familiar fishing shacks and boats.[3]

The picture is as intensely real as anything I have ever seen. You observe the boy in khaki uniform preventing the faithful from drawing near their Lord, and you ask yourself: Have *I* become part of a culture that keeps men from Christ and his Gospel? You see the cross of the unrepentant as it sways away from the Master's, and you ask: Is this what my indifference does—*to God?*

And that central cross—will it never come down? The dark sea and the tawny cliffs and the daggered lightnings hurl the words back at you—*will never come down, will never come down, will never* . . . not till wars cease

And rumored ills,
Reel to annihilation in the wrack,
And dissipate to dust along old memory's track—[4]

will never come down.

Here is indictment of the world's ancestral blindness, but here too "Something is loosed to change the shaken world."

As of old beside the glowing coals of the charcoal fire in the courtyard of the high priest's palace when our Lord turned and looked straight at Peter, and by a look melted his heart, so out of the silences that interrupt our years he looks at us, each of us with his secret grief, each of us with a memory of failure that balks the soul's high dream, and calls us to the comradeship of that cross which claims a vast discipleship as its own.

The Silence in the Courtroom

> Then Pilate said to him,
> "Do you not hear how many things they testify
> against you?" But he gave him no answer,
> not even to a single charge; so that
> the governor wondered greatly.
> Matt. 27:13-14

> This is a strange picture of Jesus.
> It makes me afraid. An austere, silent,
> judging Christ. He stands there
> before these questioning men like a statue.
> Is it possible that some day when I speak to Him,
> "questioning with Him in many words,"
> He may be as stonily silent?
> James Black, "The Dilemmas of Jesus"

Once, after a long and heated debate in Parliament, Disraeli who was then prime minister was challenged as to why he had remained silent. Disraeli replied, "It is better for men to ask why you did not speak than why you did."

Although it is customary to speak of Jesus as the Word of God, there was an hour when he memorably became the Silence of God. Repeatedly during the hours between his arrest in the Garden of Gethsemane and his Crucifixion, Jesus faced relentless questioning about himself, his Gospel, and the nature of his mission. He had ordinarily appeared eager to answer the inquiries folk put to him. But as he faces his accusers there is a silence that falls strangely like judgment on all they are and on all they represent.

He is escorted through great rooms and noble houses. Throughout his ordeal, his majesty is undiminished by the indignities he suffers as he is buffeted and abused by the rough guards.

Think of him, then, his hands bound in chains, confronting the Roman Empire in the person of the provincial governor, Pilate, and ponder the opportunity that this presented to Jesus. For if the impressive cures that Jesus wrought can be attributed to the winsome communication of vitality of one who was the personification of health, before which the neurotic and the cataleptic disorderings of personality vanished, then surely the man who stands before Pilate could have swayed any mind, had he so chosen, and deprived the opposition of its freedom to make its own subjective judgments.

"Are you the king of the Jews?"

"The words are yours."

"And what of the charges laid against you?"

But the prisoner only looks at Pilate silently. Think what difference one word might have made in Pilate's decision—*one word*.

"Do you not hear all this evidence that is brought against you?"—as if Pilate, trained in the disciplines of Roman justice, were pleading with Jesus to speak.

But for the fifth time in Jesus' last week a dramatic silence has fallen: He refuses to answer, to the governor's great astonishment.

Uncanny, the way he faces his questioners in unprotesting silence, this silent Christ. "Rather assume thy right in silence and *de facto* than voice it with claims and challenges," Francis Bacon was to say in his essay, *Of Great Place.*

You can easily imagine looking up when you hear a door open, and see Christ standing there—*but if he should not speak?* If in his eyes you read his verdict, where would you hide from his searching glance?

Why did Jesus refuse to reply to Pilate? Why was his only answer a silence that filled Pilate with astonishment? In seeking the reason, we must first examine the role in which Jesus' accusers had represented him. First, Jesus was a threat to the ancient systems of sacrifice that centered in the temple. These sacrifices had long been exploited by Annas, the deposed high priest who clung to power in the person of the present high priest, Caiaphas, his son-in-law. On the Mount of Olives were the dovecotes of Annas who made a handsome profit from the sale of doves, the sacrificial offering of the poorest of the land.[1] Then, as now, Jesus was a threat to religion when it loses the human touch.

But there was a second role in which Jesus' accusers had tried to cast him—that of the revolutionary.[2] It is curious how those who adopt violence as their desperate device still seize on the name of Jesus to find a sanction for their disruption. For Jesus' accusers, their most telling indictment was the attempt to identify him with the Zealots and the *Sicarii,* the bloody parties whose patriotism prompted them to careers in assassination. These were the men who had a knife hidden in their shirts, ready to slide it into the ribs of the first unwary Roman they met.

That anyone would believe Jesus endorsed the violence

that lay just barely concealed beneath the calm face of the province; that his Gospel had been so misconceived even by some of his own disciples, only indicates the passion of his generation for freedom and the intense frustration of its subjection to Rome. His presence, when the tide of his popularity was running high, seemed to many to embody the national hope.

I have sometimes tried to imagine the sadness of the Master at this failure, sometimes deliberate, to understand his Beatitudes. A voice like the sound of many waters is still whispering, "Oh slow of heart to believe!"

He stands there with the chains around his wrists before Pilate.

"Have you nothing to say in your defense? You see how many charges they are bringing against you."

But to Pilate's astonishment Jesus makes no further reply. Astonishment! "There is a silence that speaks!"

Why did Jesus remain silent? If the answer lies in part in who Jesus was and in who he was misconceived to be, another part of the answer lies in who Pilate was and what he had become. The glimpses the Gospels give us of Pilate display a character confirmed by historians who were his contemporaries.

"Suffered under Pontius Pilate"—this phrase that immortalizes him in the Apostles' Creed was coined, not by Christians, but by the Roman historian Tacitus (*ca.* 55-120).

Philo (20 B.C.-A.D. 50), the Jewish historian, relates that Pilate had hung in his palace in Jerusalem gilded votive shields which bore the emperor's name. This sacrilege in the holy city where only God was to be honored had so deeply incensed the devout that Tiberias had ordered Pilate to remove the shields. "Philo ascribes to Pilate rape, insult, murder, and inhumanity." [3]

Josephus cites a similar instance "when Jewish scruples were offended by troops who entered Jerusalem bearing standards with the image of the emperor on them. A crowd gathered outside Pilate's residence in Caesarea in protest; after five days Pilate had them surrounded in the race course by Roman troops, but determined to accede to their wishes rather than run the risk involved in opposing them. On another occasion, Pilate's intention to use funds from the temple treasury for construction of an aqueduct aroused a protest which was silenced by troops with bludgeons. A third incident involved the Samaritans. These, led by an impostor, promised to reveal the place of concealment on Mount Gerizim of sacred vessels supposedly stored there since the time of Moses. When the Samaritans armed and gathered at the mountain, troops dispersed them, and thereafter leading and notable Samaritans were executed. Complaint was made to the Roman legate to Syria, Vitellius, with the result that Pilate was displaced and sent to Rome." [4]

Now perhaps we are ready to determine why Jesus, hitherto so eager to answer the honest questions of sincere seekers, has only silence for the cynical governor of the province. James Black in his discussion of "The Dilemma of Silence" has some rewarding insights for all who would understand the manner of Jesus' confrontation on that fateful night:

Pilate . . . Poor Pilate! He had been reared and trained in the honored Roman traditions of justice and law. Great traditions! Great law, the foundation-stone of all modern law! Yet he twisted that iron system like a piece of putty in his supple fingers. In his weak and indifferent way, he tried to do justly. But justice needs a fearless heart and a scorn of consequences!

"Thou art no friend of Caesar, Pilate, if thou let this man go free." That settled the matter. The threat of complaint! So he delivered Jesus into their hands. Then, in a melodramatic pose, he washed his own hands. Stained hands, that water will not cleanse!

Now tell me . . . What had one like Jesus to say to one like that?

James Black concluded that there were four tempers to which Jesus refused to respond:

Jesus always refused to answer anyone who tried to trap Him.

We see this in many striking instances. Pharisees, Scribes, and lawyers came frequently with cunning questions that they might "catch" Him. . . . But on every occasion, "perceiving their wickedness," He turned their questions adroitly aside. . . .

Jesus has no answer for those who prejudge Him.

He wants us, He asks us, to judge Him. "Whom say ye that I am?" He welcomes every honest inquiry regarding Himself or His claims. But prejudging is not judging. It argues a closed mind and a shut heart. That is fatal. . . .

Jesus has no answer for a poseur.

Affectation of life or belief—(if it is ever possible to "affect" a belief; some think it is)—is at the opposite pole from the natural ways and mind of Jesus. He Himself was so perfectly sincere and real and earnest. He preached truth, and was truth. And if you will notice, the one thing that roused His anger was pretension and sham. He never had anything to say to affectation and unreality. He lashed the Pharisees, not because they were sinners, but because they were hypocrites. . . .

Jesus had no answer for a dishonest doubter.

"Whence comest thou?" said Pilate. The Roman had been told that this prisoner claimed to be the Son of God, the Messiah, a King. But Pilate, amid his broken and discredited gods, was a cynical skeptic. He regarded the "religious Jews" with a sneer. We know that he had no place in his thinking either for a life with God here or a life with God hereafter. Indeed when they spoke of the "sons of God" at Rome, it was generally with a sneer or a snigger.

When the Woman at the Well spoke to Him about the Messiah, Jesus answered simply, "I that speak unto thee am He." She had practically asked Him Pilate's question "Whence comest thou?" With a magnificent respect for her groping mind, He answered her beyond her asking.

"Whence comest thou?" asked Pilate. Jesus was silent.

Why? . . . *He deals with doubt, but not with dishonest doubt.*

This last great chance.

Will he take it?

Now they are gathered in their sweltering masses, travelers and pilgrims from many lands. The leaders of the people are there, the great men who now hold His destiny in their hands. Pilate and Herod are there. Even if He is to die, perhaps He will make a martyr's last declaration.

A dramatic message from God!

But He had reasoned with them in full measure for three years. Going in and out, He had preached God's message and Kingdom, opening up God's word and God's will. He had refused all dramatic and startling methods at the outset of His ministry. Could He begin them at the end? He wished no message delivered on the crest of passion and amid turgid emotion. Amid all this fear and passion, He Himself is now the quietest and most restrained person in Jerusalem. For after Gethsemane, the strong serene composure lasts unbroken to the end.

The day of speech is past. It is now the day of action.

His words had not won them.

Perhaps the Great Act would?

Since then, the Cross has been the world's silent sermon.[5]

The Silence of the Threefold Hour

It was now about the sixth hour,
and there was darkness over the whole
land until the ninth hour,
while the sun's light failed.
Luke 23:44-45a

And so the wounded greatness of the world
In silence lies—
And death is shattered by the light from out
Those darkened eyes.
Madeleine Caron Rock, "He Is the Lonely
Greatness of the World."

It is surely one of the astonishing details of the Gospels
that on Golgotha, the Hill of the Skull, in an hour when
soldiers cast lots for a dying man's clothes, and a rabble
stared, and passersby jeered, a dying convict on a cross
turned to Christ, his companion in crucifixion, and for the
first time of which we have a record addressed him simply
as "Jesus—Jesus, remember me when you come in your
kingly power." And Jesus answered, *"Truly, I say to you,
today you will be with me in Paradise"* (Luke 23:42-43).

It is precisely at this moment that history springs one of
its surprises: you expect someone to jeer. But the fever

dies suddenly in the faces of the soldiers flinging the dice. You expect at least a caustic rejoinder from a bystander. *Instead, there is only the light going out of the sky as the lengthening shadows of three crosses fall athwart the fearful, mute visages of the throng upon the hill.*

Pär Lagkervist, the Swedish novelist, portrays the scene through the eyes of Barabbas who is still stunned as he tries to comprehend the amnesty he has been offered:

But all at once the whole hill grew dark, as though the light had gone out of the sun; it was almost pitch-dark, and in the darkness above, the crucified man cried in a loud voice:
—My God, my God, why hast thou forsaken me?
It sounded horrible. Whatever did he mean? And why had it grown so dark? It was the middle of the day. It was quite unaccountable. The three crosses were just faintly visible up there. It looked weird. Something terrible was surely going to happen. The soldiers had leaped to their feet and grabbed their weapons; whatever happened, they always rushed for their weapons.[1]

The darkness that shrouds Calvary from mortal eyes from midday until three o'clock is another of the dramatic silences of our Lord's last week. It is as if God would enfold in a torrent of darkness an event which it would be too terrible to look upon and live. There is no voice from heaven. There is no deliverance from the Cross. There is no miracle to confound the enemies of Jesus. All this we can understand, for we have learned to do without miracles. But God help us if we ever refuse to keep looking into "the sorrow of the threefold hour" and trying to penetrate its mystery.

Once when a film was being shown which depicted the life of Christ, the audience was hushed as the Crucifixion scene reached its climax. One man was deeply moved as he saw Christ being led away to be crucified. But at this moment a girl sitting in front of him turned to a companion and said, "Let's go—this is the place where we came in." The man who was intent upon Christ was shocked by the casual way in which the girl seemed to dismiss the portrayal of what for him was the most sacred hour in history. Then it dawned on him that what the girl had said is literally true: the Cross of Jesus Christ *is* the place where we come in.

The Cross is the place where we discover that God has given himself for us in a great redemption. But for the silence and the darkness of the threefold hour when time seemed to stop, we might never have peered into this mystery far enough to find the very heart of God.

There are facts in astronomy which can only be ascertained when the sun is in total eclipse. They are true always, and affect the conditions under which we never cease to live; but they can be perceived only during that minute or two of which most of us have an experience only once during a life-time.[2]

As David Grayson observed, "Without darkness, man would have been vastly longer in discovering himself and his universe without darkness, how see the stars?"[3]

In his book, *The Black Hills,* Robert Casey relates his memory of seeing the Spearfish Passion Play

exactly one week before Hitler concluded his nonaggression pact with Russia. The air was frosty as it sometimes gets in the hills on a night in mid-August. The sky had been cloudy all day and in the middle of the trial scene the rain came with a stiff wind behind it. In the courtyard of Pilate's palace the howling mob was getting wet to the hide—as was the audience. The Roman cavalry leaned convincingly against the gale and a flood of water from the hill began to sluice around the governor's doorstep. . . . Down from the dais before Pilate came the Christus while the mob yelled, "Crucify Him!" loudly enough to raise an echo in the hills behind the ampitheater.

. . . . The veil of the rain under the big spotlights gave it a ghostly, intangible quality—unearthly and beyond the scope of one's imagination. And yet it was the most convincing drama I have ever seen. This ghastly injustice might not be taking place in my world. But it was certainly taking place somewhere else, in some other world—the world we were looking at.

The Christus shouldered his cross and began to stagger up the muddy road to Golgotha and presently there were three pathetically white and frail-looking figures hanging to the three crosses on a hillock that the dim, wet light made seem far away—then suddenly the stage went black. The amphitheater lights went on. And there an audience of about five hundred people were standing up absolutely motionless looking into blind night with the rain beating into their eyes. . . . In a moment they stirred as I did, like people who had been asleep. And everybody filed silently out.[4]

What does the silence at Calvary mean? It means stumbling upon God. It means vision. It means a power is loosed that pours contempt on all our pride and exposes us to the winds of God before which none in his own strength shall stand. Above the hills of time the Cross stands "like a signpost for free travelers," urging on us awareness of the God who saves, holding us fast in the spell of a silence that speaks redemption.

The time will never be when we shall not need silences as awesome as the darkness that descended on Calvary to recall us to ourselves and to all that God means us to be.

Sometimes just as we have come to accept "the withering away of the Cross," a silence falls . . . darkness, . . . and it strikes us how mortal we are and that before three decades have passed, or four, our very names will be unremembered and all we strive for as if it had never been.

Then there rises out of the silence the recollection of his Cross and of that other hour. We strive to get ahead in the world, but as I once heard it put, "There isn't room for all of us at the top: the only place where there is room for all of us is at the foot of the Cross." [5] If we reflect, we know that it is here that God has given himself to us in a great and saving act.

Yes, and it is here where at last we find the courage to address him with the same desperate familiarity with which a man just beyond his reach—yet *not* beyond his reach— dares to plead, "Jesus, remember me when you come in your kingly power.' Remember me! For if you do not remember me, I shall go down to the dust bereft and unremembered of all.

We never know the hour when his Cross will come our way. In Coventry they still tell the story of the bomb that leveled the historic cathedral. When the handsome modern cathedral was completed, it struck the bishop that a new church, however impressive it might be, was vain unless there was also a renewal of the community in Christ that gathered there.

Out of a solemn rededication of the clergy and laity, out of retreats and periods of prayer, Coventry was reborn. This new birth extended to all the outlying churches of the diocese. But—how to embody this invisible presence of the Holy Spirit and make it memorably real? The Cross was the answer. The ancient wrought nails which had been fashioned by hand in the Middle Ages when the cathedral was built were found in great numbers in the charred ruins, and from these a cross of nails was fashioned.

As the spirit of Christ worked its renewal in the hearts of a chastened people, men and boys bore this cross of nails from one parish to the next and passed it on with a deeply solemn realization that they were truly members one of another in the Body of Christ. For forty days and forty nights they bore the cross, supported by a continuous chain of prayer. One who had witnessed this procession of the cross of nails recalled that

as the cross was delivered into the hand of the priest of the receiving company, the first priest said in a loud voice "CHRIST REIGNS."

Then followed the prayer "Almighty God, . . . grant that we, walking in the way of the cross, may find it none other than the way of life and peace."

This was followed by silence. The cross was raised aloft . . . and we took the cross further on its pilgrimage.[6]

"Silence . . . and we took the cross further"—this is the way each generation in Christ is introduced to the love of God.

E. B. White concludes his captivating study of New York City with the description of a tree:

A block or two west of the new City of Man in Turtle Bay there is an old willow tree that presides over an interior garden. It is a battered tree, long suffering and much climbed, held together by strands of wire but beloved of those who know it. In a way it symbolizes the city: life under difficulties, growth against odds, saprise in the midst of concrete, and the steady reaching for the sun. Whenever I look at it nowadays, and feel the cold shadow of the planes, I think, "This must be saved, this particular thing, this very tree." If it were to go, all would go—this city, this mischievous and marvelous monument which not to look upon would be like death.[7]

There is a Tree, "mystical and eternal" which rises above the hills of time. Where its shadow falls, there God's claim rests upon us and something is exacted of us. Those who have entered even a little way into the silence of the threefold hour are bound to say, "This must be saved, this particular thing, this very tree."

The three hours of darkness are past. Then Jesus, crying with a loud voice, ended the silence with, *"Father, into thy hands I commend my spirit."*

Then silence again.

They would have to wait until Easter before the silence ended.

The Silence on the Street of Splendid Strangers

When he was at table with them,
he took the bread and blessed,
and broke it, and gave it to them. And
their eyes were opened and they recognized him;
and he vanished out of their sight.
Luke 24:30-31

Out of one darkness the travellers have
come to be taken into another, but for a moment
one sees their faces, awful and still,
all uplifted .... This is all: their words have
vanished, all memory of the movements
they made then has also vanished: one remembers
only their silence and their still faces lifted in
the phantasmal light of lost time.
Thomas Wolfe, "Of Time and the River"

Few scenes in the Gospel make a greater appeal than Emmaus Road as it winds between the terraced vineyards. The waves of heat that shimmer above its golden dust lie heavy on the hearts of Cleopas and his companion as they put Jerusalem behind them. Emmaus ahead . . . the lonely house standing back from the road . . . nightfall.

There is that in the story—and it is easy to believe that a greater than Luke put it there—that haunts and thrills you. As you read, you keep looking over your shoulder as if you had heard a footfall. For the house you are thinking about at the end of the road is *your* house, and the road stretching away a parable of *your* life. You are almost choked with the beauty of the story. You know the surprise at the end of it, yet it is always new. For it may be that there have been hours when you, too, have walked the Street of Splendid Strangers.[1]

Did you notice that when the stranger overtook them, they never saw his shadow on the road? The road wound in and out among the little hills, but they never saw his shadow on the road. Afterward they could not remember where it was the stranger had overtaken them—or when he had *not* been with them. And—did you mark?—they failed to ask him his name.

Their minds were still numb with the recollection of the dead, limp body of Jesus which Joseph of Arimathea had removed from the Cross. Once they had dared to think of Jesus as the hope of the world. Now all that remained was a legend of a vision of angels which a woman had professed to see through her tears.

The stranger kept pace with them—or slowed his pace to theirs—putting to them a thoughtful question now and then, until they poured out to him their sense of loss. Then it was he spoke a word about their Friend as if his Cross had been the lych-gate to his glory.

They were turning in at the gate now. It was there the stranger appeared to be going further, but they cannot bear to part company with him. They call after him, and he returns and joins them at table.

Was it here that the stranger paused briefly, as if the

bread reminded him of something that had happened at another table, back in another world of space and time? Cleopas and his companion had not been in the Upper Room the night that other loaf was broken, but they *saw* and they *knew*. Was there something about the way he broke the loaf—as if it were sacred, as all bread is? Or a familiar gesture they would never forget? Or the glimpse of a hand which had known the print of a nail? Or the touch of his hand on theirs when he gave them the bread? For it seemed the most natural thing in the world that the stranger should have been the host at their table.

A silence falls over the table. No one moves. Cleopas' lips are parted but he does not speak. It is the last of the dramatic silences of our Lord's last week. They *knew* him. The stranger has disappeared, but in communion with him at their own table, he has left upon their inner eye the glimpse of the risen Master. It does not matter that now they cannot hear his voice or see his face: he is alive, and the Street of Splendid Strangers has become the highway of an unbroken communion with one in whom death is being swallowed up in life. The resurrection of Christ is the assurance of God's personal response to hearts that reach out if haply they may find him. What Cleopas and his companion found under their own humble roof was a silence—but it was the silence of eternity interpreted by love.

It is not always so that silence overtakes us. A friend of mine likes to tell of the day when he was walking along a deserted city street in the dusk. Presently he began to hear the sound of footsteps behind him. The apprehension rose on his mind that someone was following him. He looked up and down the street. There was no one there. He turned a corner and walked on, but the steps of someone relentlessly pursuing him filled him with cold fear. Then he made a discovery: he had that day purchased a hearing aid, and he suddenly realized that he was listening for the first time in many years—to his own footsteps.

Now, imagine for a moment that you are in a world where you are solitary and God is dead. No voice speaks to your conscience. No ideal lifts a beckoning finger like a pillar of cloud by day or of fire by night. No love enfolds you. No mercy lays its mantle over your sins.

Down a straight road you walk, with no sound falling on your ears except the sound of your own footfall—you, completely alone, walking in a vast silence in a dead world in which you have lost your way. Do you know what would happen? You would go mad and lose your last thread of contact with reality before many hours had passed.

In 1949 the United States Army Signal Corps perfected what it called "a silent chamber" to measure the noise of army field equipment. Army engineers entered this silent chamber to test the effect of "silence—dead, absolute silence. Have you ever wondered what it would be like? Not the stillness of a quiet room, but no noise at all. . . . Thirty minutes of absolute silence was just about all anyone could stand. After thirty minutes the engineers became uneasy. After a few hours, the army said, the dead silence 'produced adverse psychological effects.' " [2]

"A voice, not our voice but a voice coming from something not ourselves, in the existence of which we cannot disbelieve" [3]—this is not only necessary for our health: it is the ground for our celebration of Easter. What we hear in the hour of our guilt is not our own footfall, but "those strong Feet that followed, followed after." [4] What we hear in the hour of our grief is not the throbbing of our own heart, but the heartbeat of him who loved us and gave himself for us.

To thoughtful and devout minds in our very different age the objection will surely occur: how is the resurrection of Jesus Christ available to men of faith today? For we simply do not visualize the presence of God in our midst in the manner in which the Gospels introduce the supernatural. Part of the reason for this is the fact of Jesus himself. He has so grown upon our hearts that if we seek God at all, we are most apt to realize him in all that happens in our midst that is deeply personal.

Therefore we are not in the habit of visualizing an angel descending from heaven and rolling back the stone that guards the entrance to a tomb. We do not know what to make of the disappearance of the physical body of Jesus. And, as we would expect when we are dealing with events that seem to be at home both in the world the five senses report and the world of spirit that lies beyond them or penetrates them, we suffer great perplexity; how shall we account for the appearances in which the risen Christ manifests himself, sometimes physical, as if he had borne the scars of the Cross into the eternal world; sometimes disembodied, as one who comes, the doors being shut?

All of this inevitably fills us with a sense of mystery, for it is on the whole unlike the nature of the realities we experience today. It is therefore not to be wondered at that even thoughtful men of faith are troubled by an event in which they desire with all their hearts to believe.

A beginning in comprehending the Resurrection might

be made in reflecting on a curious motif that occurs in the recognition scenes in which the Gospels recount the appearances of our risen Lord: "It is striking that one characteristic of Jesus' apparitions is that no one recognized him immediately." [5]

Let us see if we can reconstruct the typical stories the early Christians liked to relate of their experiences of the risen Christ, omitting for the moment the supernatural dimension with which faith afterward imbued them; for as the Gospels plainly indicate, so casual were the encounters that became the basis for their eventual communion with their risen Lord that it was only in the final moments of a chance meeting with a stranger—or indeed afterward, when they reflected on the meaning of their encounter— that they became indubitably convinced that Christ had been in their midst.

Here, for example, is Mary Magdalene coming down the path to the garden tomb. It is scarcely daybreak, and certainly a time and a place to arouse her apprehensions. She stands there, just outside the tomb, perplexed because it has been opened, and someone has borne away the body of the most wonderful person she has ever known.

She turns away from the tomb, but there is no one but a gardener standing there. He must have been the kindest of gardeners, because he is at once sympathetic and asks why she is weeping, and who it is she seeks. She does not recognize him and pleads, "Sir, if you have carried him away, tell me where you have laid him, and I will take him away."

But now the gardener recognizes her and calls her— tenderly, I think—by name, "Mary." It is odd how our sympathies can shape a word and endow it with a rush of understanding that reaches out to touch the brokenness and loneliness of another's grief; odd how the air about us can receive the impression of our compassion, and put the strong arm of a gracious charity about the shoulders of another—or, as in the case of Mary Magdalene, summon her to a new dignity of winsome womanliness.

Was it so, in communion with the gardener, that she began to be aware of her risen Lord? Is it possible that his availability to his own that first Easter is of exactly the same order as his availability to us today? If we truly believe in his resurrection, is it because we have found that where two or three gather in love and in the mutuality of faith, there he is sure to be in the midst?

Again, here are Cleopas and his companion plodding along Emmaus road. A wayfarer overtakes them. So far as they know, they have never seen him before, but in the most natural way they fall into conversation about what troubles them most. They relate the sad events of which the wayfarer appears not to have heard, but in a singular way the wayfarer understands, and shares with them his own belief that Christ must needs suffer these things and enter into his glory.

Now they are drawing near to Emmaus. The wayfarer appears to be going further, but the communion the three of them have had is too perfect to be broken. It is around their table at the evening meal that there rises on their minds, out of the deep communion they have known, the solemn persuasion that the spirit of God is upon them. After the wayfarer has gone, "their eyes are opened," and the astonished admission they make to each other rings in our faith ever since: "Did not our hearts burn within us while he talked to us on the road, while he opened to us the scriptures?"

Again the scene shifts and we are on the seacoast at Tiberias. Tired fishermen are returning cold and wet in the dismal first light of morning after a fruitless night on the sea. As they begin to put in to shore, they see someone on the beach whom they do not recognize. He has seen them first, and has taken the trouble to find some charcoal so that he may kindle a fire.

Presently he straightens up and shouts the greeting you always put to a fisherman, "Any fish?"

"No," they answer.

"Cast the net to starboard, and you'll have a catch," the stranger suggests, and bends down to tend his fire.

Presently they are pulling a big haul of fish into the boat.

"Bring some fish and come and have breakfast," the stranger calls. As they approach the shore, and reflect that someone who need not have bothered has had the kindness to anticipate their hunger and to kindle a fire, suddenly, in a burst of recognition, the Beloved Disciple exclaims to Peter, "It is the Lord!"

As simply as this the risen Master makes his presence known. If, in retelling these stories, I have arbitrarily stripped away the supernatural element that inevitably added a new dimension to the lives of men and women for whom the resurrection faith afterward became the gladness and the glory of new beings in Christ; and if I have portrayed Christ in his risen greatness becoming manifest to his followers in deeply personal and casual encounters, it is because this is the way the Gospels report the manner in which he began to be known as risen from the dead.

His resurrection became a reality available to them when they met the most ordinary people—a wayfarer, a gardener, a stranger, who took the trouble to kindle a fire and minister to their needs. Is it not in such communions as these that the reality of the risen life becomes eternally available to us? And therefore we call anyone common at our peril.

The hungry man slowly climbed the steps and opened the door of the church. There was weariness evident in every step he took. He had been sleeping under the stars for several frosty nights, and his face had the leathery look of a man familiar with all weathers. He had the look of a man who had had to make do for a very long time.

"You couldn't let a man have a dollar for a meal?"

It happened that a group was about to take potluck in the dining room, and I invited the hungry man to break bread with us. All through the meal he kept his coat buttoned closely as if he wanted to store all the heat he could before he took up his journey in the bitter cold. I filled his plate with warm food, and we sat down at the end of a table by ourselves.

"How long have you been on the road?" I asked the hungry man.

"A long time," he said, "a very long time."

"And it never occurred to you to settle down and take some steady work?"

"No," he said, "I used to be a carpenter. But I'm one of those who has to be on his way. I'd never be happy settled in just one place."

It was odd the way he said it—like the wayfarer who visited Emmaus and who made as if he would have gone further until Cleopas and his companion invited him to stay for supper.

"What do you call yourself?" I asked the hungry man.

"I'm Mr. Immanuel," he said.

"Do you know what the name Immanuel means?"

He looked at me quizzically as if he knew I was going to supply the answer myself.

"Immanuel," I said, "means 'God-with-us.' You are Mr. God-with-us."

He looked at me fixedly now, and it struck me that his shoulders were bowed as if he had been carrying heavy burdens for a very long time.

"Don't you forget," I said when I shook his hand as he was leaving. "Remember that you're Mr. God-with-us."

He did not smile or take amiss what I had said about his name. Presently he said his thanks and was off on his lonely journey that has no ending. And I thought: He still goes on his way, the hungry man, Mr. God-with-us, in his shabby coat, and always a look in his eyes as if he would go further. But when he had gone, my heart began to burn within me, and I had no doubt that Cleopas and his companion, in that silence that suddenly fell over their table, would have understood.

Notes

I

1. Heinrich Heine, "Germany after Luther," quoted by C. J. Hambro in *How to Win the Peace* (New York: Lippincott, 1942), pp. 59-60.
2. "Prophet of Hope and Fear," *Time,* 18 October 1954, p. 108.
3. Norman Nicholson, "The Ride to Jerusalem."

II

1. William Blake, "My Spectre around me night and day," stanza 14.
2. Paul Scherer, in *The Interpreter's Bible,* Vol. VIII (Nashville: Abingdon Press, 1952), p. 339.

III

1. Quoted by Leslie Weatherhead in *It Happened in Palestine* (New York: Abingdon Press, 1936), p. 195.
2. H. V. Morton, *In the Steps of the Master* (New York: Dodd, Mead, 1934), p. 405.
3. David Smith, *The Days of His Flesh* (New York: Harper and Brothers, 8th ed. rev., n.d.), p. 455.
4. *Ibid.,* p. 459.

IV

1. Werner Heisenberg, *Physics and Beyond,* tr. Arnold J. Pomerans (New York: Harper, 1970), as quoted by Elting Morison in a review in *New York Times,* 17 January 1971, p. 31.
2. J. A. Findlay, *A Portrait of Peter* (Nashville: Abingdon Press, 1935), p. 128.

3. Some of the language is borrowed from an interpretation of the picture when it was displayed in 1936 in the First Methodist Church, Chatham, Mass.
4. Amos Niven Wilder, "L'envoi" in *Arachne* (New Haven: Yale University Press, 1928), p. 85.

V

1. "It would seem . . . from a note in Derenbourg (*Histoire de la Palestine,* 467) that the sale of doves was a monopoly of . . . the powerful family of Annas, who sold them to retailers from bazaars kept by them on Mount Olivet." Cunningham Geike, *The Life and Words of Christ,* Vol. I (New York: D. Appleton, 1891), p. 561, note *h*.
2. For a convincing argument against the identification of Jesus with violence, see Oscar Cullmann, *Jesus and the Revolutionaries* (New York: Harper, 1970).
3. Samuel Sandmel, "Pilate, Pontius," in *The Interpreter's Dictionary of the Bible* (Nashville: Abingdon Press, 1962), p. 811.
4. *Ibid.,* p. 811.
5. James Black, *The Dilemmas of Jesus* (London: Fleming H. Revell, 1925), pp. 171-78.

VI

1. Pär Lagkervist, *Barabbas,* tr. Alan Blair (New York: Random House, 1951), pp. 9-10.
2. E. F. Scott, *The Book of Revelation* (New York: Scribner's, 1940), p. 151.
3. David Grayson, *Under My Elm* (Garden City, N.Y.: Doubleday, 1942), p. 197.
4. Robert Casey: *The Black Hills,* (New York: Bobbs Merrill, 1949), pp. 281-82.
5. Richard Roberts.
6. Stephen Verney, *Fire in Coventry* (London: Hodder and Stoughton, 1964), p. 38.
7. E. B. White, *Here Is New York* (New York: Harper and Brothers, 1949), pp. 53-54.

VII

1. The phrase is used by G. K. Chesterton in *Orthodoxy.*
2. An experiment reported by Associated Press in *Binghampton Press,* 13 April, 1949, p. 29.
3. Quoted by John A. Mackay, *A Preface to Christian Theology* (New York: Macmillan, 1941), p. 18.
4. Francis Thompson, "The Hound of Heaven."
5. Louis Evely, *The Gospels Without Myth* (Garden City, N.Y.: Doubleday, 1971), p. 161.